ANIMAL EXTREMES

DEEPEST DIVERS

BY ELISABETH NORTON

WWW.APEXEDITIONS.COM

Apex is distributed by North Star Editions:
sales@northstareditions.com | 888-417-0195

Produced for Apex by Red Line Editorial.

Photographs ©: Shutterstock Images, cover, 4–5, 6–7, 8, 9, 10–11, 12–13, 14–15, 16–17, 29; NOAA Office of Ocean Exploration and Research/NOAA, 1, 24, 25; Danté Fenolio/Science Source, 18–19; Herve Chaumeton/Science Source, 20; NOAA Ocean Exploration/NOAA, 22–23; Hidden Ocean/NOAA, 26; iStockphoto, 27

Library of Congress Control Number: 2022919882

ISBN
978-1-63738-529-6 (hardcover)
978-1-63738-583-8 (paperback)
978-1-63738-690-3 (ebook pdf)
978-1-63738-637-8 (hosted ebook)

Printed in the United States of America
Mankato, MN
082023

NOTE TO PARENTS AND EDUCATORS

Apex books are designed to build literacy skills in striving readers. Exciting, high-interest content attracts and holds readers' attention. The text is carefully leveled to allow students to achieve success quickly. Additional features, such as bolded glossary words for difficult terms, help build comprehension.

CHAPTER 1

WATCHING WHALES

A boat floats in the ocean near North Carolina. It carries several scientists. They are looking for Cuvier's beaked whales.

Scientists who study ocean animals are called marine biologists.

The scientists want to study how deep the whales dive. So, they find several whales and put tracking tags on them.

Scientists sometimes use long poles to place tracking tags on the bodies of whales.

TRACKING TAGS

A tracking tag shows an animal's location. The tag sends **signals** to a **satellite**. The satellite sends information to computers. Scientists study this information. They can see where and when the animal moves.

Cuvier's beaked whales use their strong, wide tails to dive beneath the water.

One whale goes 9,816 feet (2,992 m) deep. That's the deepest dive made by a **mammal**. Another whale makes the longest dive. Its dive lasts 3 hours and 42 minutes.

Cuvier's beaked whales spend very little time above water. This makes them hard for scientists to study.

FAST FACT

Like all mammals, whales need air. They come up to the **surface** to breathe.

CHAPTER 2

DIVING DOWN

Many ocean animals breathe air. Some can hold their breath a long time. Elephant seals can dive for up to two hours. They can dive more than 6,560 feet (2,000 m) deep.

Elephant seals are named for their large noses.

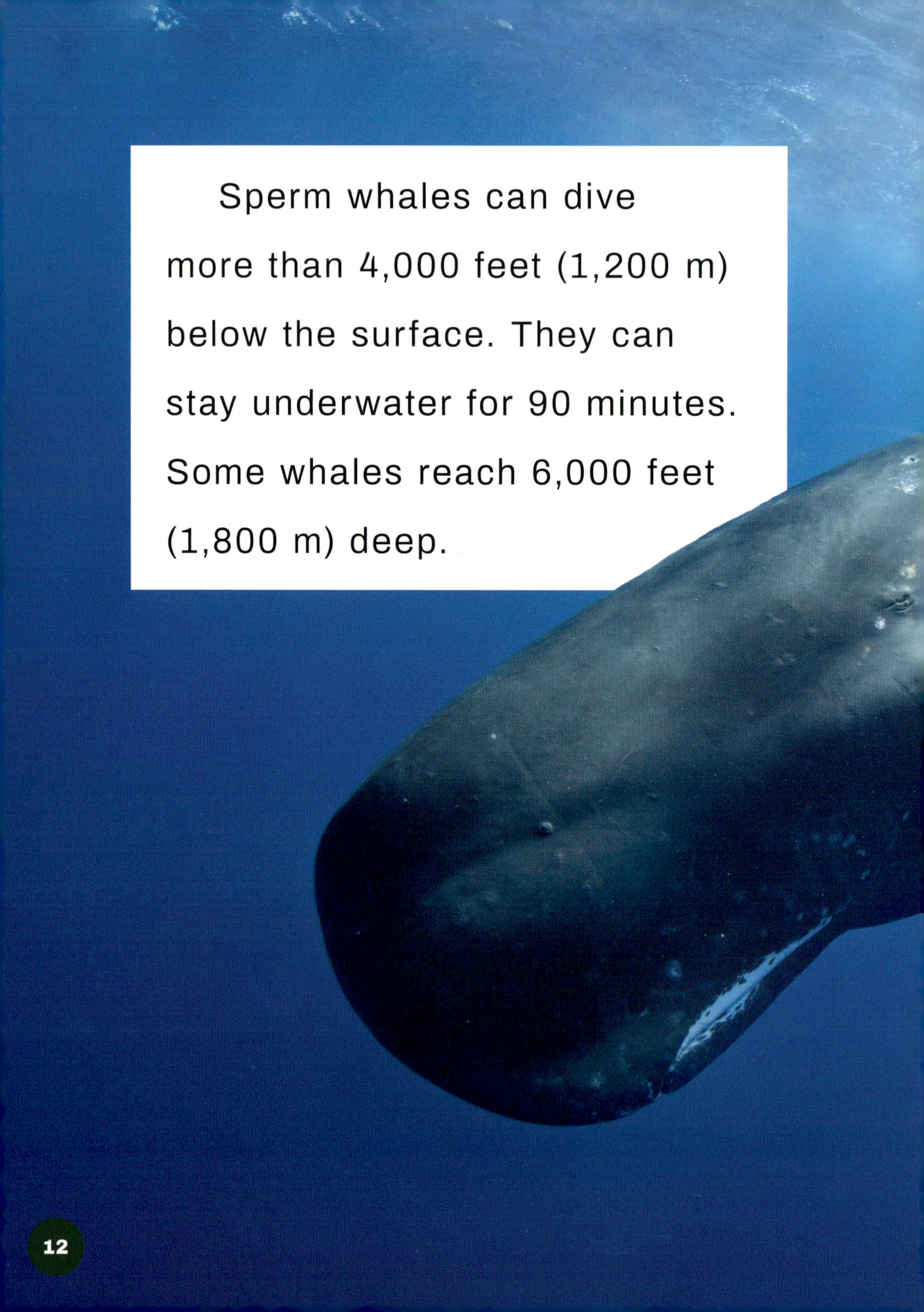

Sperm whales can dive more than 4,000 feet (1,200 m) below the surface. They can stay underwater for 90 minutes. Some whales reach 6,000 feet (1,800 m) deep.

Sperm whales dive to search for food. They often hunt squid and fish.

BIG BRAINS

A sperm whale's large body helps it store **oxygen** as it dives. The whale has a big head, too. In fact, it has the largest brain of any animal ever.

Emperor penguins are the deepest-diving birds. They can dive down more than 1,640 feet (500 m).

Emperor penguins hunt and dive in freezing water near Antarctica.

FAST FACT
Emperor penguins can hold their breath for up to 27 minutes.

CHAPTER 3

DEEP DWELLERS

The deepest-diving fish is the whale shark. Whale sharks often swim in shallow water. But they can dive up to 6,000 feet (1,800 m) deep.

Whale sharks live in warm oceans all over the world.

Some fish spend most of their time deep underwater. Sloane's viperfish can swim down to 3,280 feet (1,000 m). Water here is dark and cold.

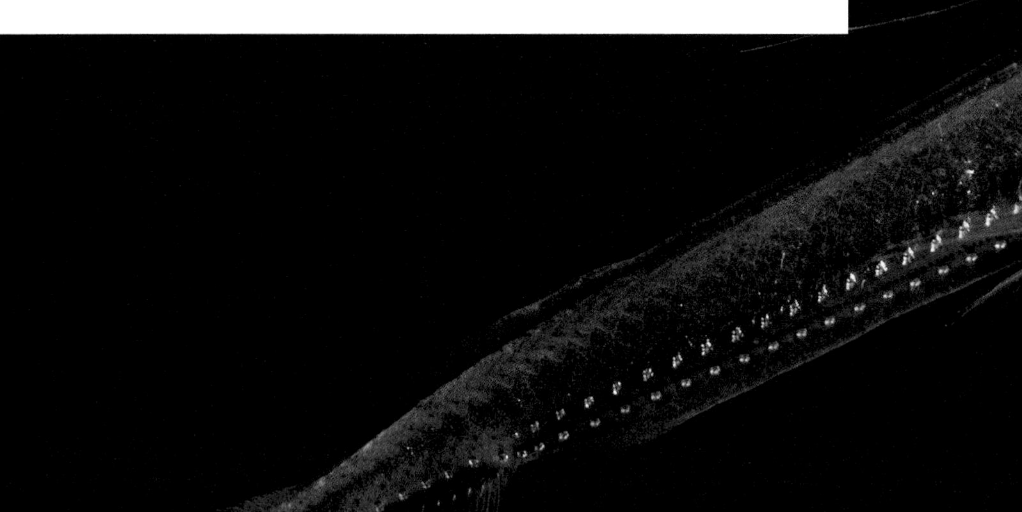

A Sloane's viperfish has a line of flashing lights along the side of its body.

FAST FACT

Parts of a viperfish's body glow in the dark. This helps the fish catch **prey**.

Bristlemouth fish are named for their very sharp teeth.

Bristlemouth fish can live even deeper. They swim 1,640 to 5,000 feet (500–1,500 m) below the surface.

DEEP-DIVING RAYS

Chilean devil **rays** usually swim near the ocean's surface. But they sometimes make deep dives. One ray dove 6,062 feet (1,848 m) deep. Scientists think rays may dive to find food.

CHAPTER 4

NEAR THE SEAFLOOR

Some animals swim way down near the seafloor. One bigfin squid was found more than 20,000 feet (6,100 m) deep.

A bigfin squid can grow to be 21 feet (6.4 m) long.

Some octopuses dive even deeper. Scientists saw one octopus nearly 23,000 feet (7,000 m) below the surface. And one jellyfish was spotted 32,800 feet (10,000 m) down.

Scientists think the deepest-diving octopus was a Dumbo octopus.

Several types of Crossota jellyfish can live in the deep sea.

FAST FACT

Scientists know more about the moon and Mars than about the seafloor.

Snailfish are small fish with soft bodies.

Two types of snailfish live in the deepest part of the ocean. One was found 26,720 feet (8,144 m) deep.

UNDER PRESSURE

Water presses against the things it touches. As animals go deeper into the ocean, more water is above them. So, the pressure increases. Their bodies must **adapt** to **withstand** it.

The Mariana Trench is the deepest part of the Pacific Ocean. It's almost 7 miles (11 km) deep.

COMPREHENSION QUESTIONS

Write your answers on a separate piece of paper.

1. Write a few sentences describing some of the animals found in deep water near the seafloor.
2. Would you want to study animals that live in the deep ocean? Why or why not?
3. Which mammal can dive the deepest?
   - **A.** sperm whale
   - **B.** Cuvier's beaked whale
   - **C.** elephant seal
4. How would glowing in the dark help a viperfish catch prey?
   - **A.** The light could make the viperfish easier to see.
   - **B.** The light could scare away other animals.
   - **C.** The prey might see the light and swim closer.

5. What does **shallow** mean in this book?

Whale sharks often swim in ***shallow*** *water. But they can dive up to 6,000 feet (1,800 m) deep.*

A. not deep
B. not far
C. not real

6. What does **increases** mean in this book?

As animals go deeper into the ocean, more water is above them. So, the pressure ***increases****.*

A. gets brighter
B. gets stronger
C. gets less strong

Answer key on page 32.

GLOSSARY

adapt

To change to fit a particular situation.

mammal

An animal that has hair and produces milk for its young.

oxygen

A type of gas that animals need to breathe to survive.

prey

Animals that are hunted and eaten by other animals.

rays

Types of fish that have wide, flat bodies.

satellite

A device that orbits Earth, often to send or collect information.

signals

Ways of sending information from one device to another.

surface

The top of the water.

withstand

To be able to deal with or survive something.

BOOKS

Lim, Angela. *Giant Squid*. Mendota Heights, MN: Apex Editions, 2022.

London, Martha. *Deep-Sea Drones*. Minneapolis: Abdo Publishing, 2021.

Troup, Roxanne. *Deep-Sea Creatures*. New York: Enslow Publishing, 2020.

ONLINE RESOURCES

Visit **www.apexeditions.com** to find links and resources related to this title.

ABOUT THE AUTHOR

Elisabeth Norton is originally from the United States. Now she lives with her family in Switzerland, where she is an English teacher and writer.

INDEX

ANSWER KEY:
1. Answers will vary; 2. Answers will vary; 3. B; 4. C; 5. A; 6. B